Scared to be Me

How to step past fear and achieve your goals and dreams.

Beth Parris

No part of this book may be reproduced, or stored in a retrieval system, or transmitted in any form or by any means, electronic, mechanical, photocopying, recording, or otherwise, without express written permission of the publisher.

Copyright © 2020 Beth Parris

All rights reserved.

ISBN: 9798562829382

TO MY DAUGHTER

You came into my life and gave me the motivation to want more, be more and have more. Thank you for coming into my life.

1 INTRODUCTION 1
2 BEFORE TEENS..4
3 THE TEEN AGE YEARS 12
4 MY FAVORED SISTER 20
5 MOVING IN WITH DAD 26
6 MY BEST-FRIEND TURNED HUSBAND.............30
7 MARRIED LIFE...36
8 THE MOVIE 40
9 THE MEAN BOSS: FIRST PREGNANCY 44
10 SECOND PREGNANCY 52
11 MARRIED SINGLE MOM.......................................64
12 STARTED EXERCISING 68
13 THE PARTIES..76
14 PACK AND LEAVE! (1 OF 3)...................................84
15 PACK AND LEAVE! (2 OF 3) 90
16 PACK AND LEAVE! 3 OF 3 96
17 NO BIRTHDAY GIFT 104
18 THE BREAK-UP 112
19 AFTER THE BREAK-UP 118
20 UPDATE ON MY LIFE 124
21 YOU ARE IN CHARGE 128

ACKNOWLEDGMENTS

I want to thank my best-friend for being there for me when I needed it the most. He always encouraged me with my story I need to write a book.

1 INTRODUCTION

Your dreams are on the outside of fear and you must be willing to take that step into the unknown. When you step past fear, you step into achieving your goals and dreams. I say this from personal experience because I was comfortable with fear. I always wanted more, and I knew I could achieve more but the fear of putting myself out there and not believing in me kept me imprisoned for years. I am currently on the path to my dreams; I have not achieved them all yet, but I am on the path to achieving them.

Scared to be me is a true story of my life where I share my past and where I came from to be the person I am today.

This book not only contains my personal story but also the different steps I took to achieve certain things in my life.

The goal of this book is to show you how I moved from a horrible past with low self-esteem to loving myself and being confident to start my business, a YouTube channel and a podcast along with leaving a controlling husband.

This book is not made to point fingers at the people that did me wrong but to help those people out there that had a painful past and do not know how to confront the pain to overcome it so you can step into the amazing person you were meant to be.

I hope my story reaches those people that need it and that it helps you in whatever area in your life that you have the most fears and self-doubt.

Kindly note all names used in the book are fake because this book is not meant to shame people in public but to help the person that needs it.

2 BEFORE TEENS

I was born on a small island to a mentally ill mother and an extremely sweet father. My father and mother broke up before I turned 2 years old, but I never knew why they broke up, all I can remember is not seeing my mother anymore at the house.

How my mother became mentally ill you might ask, well it is because when my mother was 6 years old, her father killed her mother; he hanged her mother in the middle of the front house and woke up all the children and showed them their mother hanging from the roof with her tongue hanging from her mouth.

This incident damaged my mother's brothers and sisters in so many ways; those who have not turned crazy/mentally ill suffer from some sort of fear that they don't even know is there.

I have one memory with my mother and father together when I was a baby and I was sleeping on a mattress on the floor between the 2 of them, and when I opened my eyes, I was terrified of my mother because she had a nasty burn on her face which she received when she got my crazy uncle mad and he threw hot water in her face which made her face very ugly and I was terrified when I woke up in the middle of the night. This is the last and only time I can remember my father and mother together.

My next memory is living in a tiny 2-bedroom house with my father, his 2 brothers, and my grandmother. Every morning when both my sister and I were in bed, we would sing out loud and slow 'I want my tea teaaaaa' repeatedly which would drive my father crazy and he would fret which made us do it more because our father never shouted at us and was really fun, so we knew that if we annoyed him, the only thing he would say was 'cheese-on man, I making de tea' which was followed by a really long stupse, which made me and my sister giggle silently because it was so funny. My father moved out with his new girlfriend leaving me and my sister with my grandmother and uncles, before my sister started school.

When I was 2 years old, my sister started school and I hated being home without her, so I cried all day until she came home. This got really frustrating for my Grandmother and she got me into school the moment I turned 3 years old.

Since my mother was mentally ill, I was raised by my beautiful Grandmother and my good Uncle and they were my parents. My uncle had his own family, but he lived with us and disciplined us when needed. My grandmother was loving and caring; she did all she could to make sure that both I and my sister got the love and care we deserved from a mother. I used to love listening to all her stories about school and the Pit-Toilet Rats' ha-ha, they had a song for them, but I can't remember it now.

I lived in a small 2-bedroom, one-bathroom government house with my grandmother, my sister, 2 uncles, and 2 cousins. One of those cousins used to steal all our stuff, including our nice undies that were bought for us, and I went to school sometimes with panties that if I did participate in running, they would start to come down, so I had to sit and watch the other children as they played. But life was still sweet because I always had my grandmother to rely on and she always made sure we did not go to school without all the necessary things. So, if something were stolen, she would buy it back for us. Plus, our cousin that stole never stayed out of jail long enough to be a bother to us since I was 3 years old until I turned 12 years old.

My uncle that was like my father was nice and used to take us for drives to his friends' houses and into town on his days off. He took care of us, making sure we went to school, and we had money each day.

My other uncle was a mean, unhappy bully. He used

to put the phone beside him whenever he was home to enable him to answer our calls and hang up on our friends when they call. He would sit by the phone, and when it rang, he would pick it up and put it down or slam it down, and on the occasion that he answered, he would shout 'DON'T CALL BACK' or he would look at us straight in the eye and shout 'NOT HERE'! He knew that this tormented us and he did it more and more knowing that we couldn't do him anything since we were only children. So, we would go outside to get away from him. Now, you might say what is the big deal about him sitting by the phone and not letting us use it? This was before cell phones and we could only use land phones to communicate with friends outside of school knowing full well that our grandmother did not like us going outside much. So being stuck in the house, we would go on the telephone and talk to our friends from school. My sister and I loved being inside, so being on the phone was perfect. Once our grandmother was present in the front house, he could not do that to us or if our good uncle was there.

This mean uncle used to call us sluts and whores and would tell us 'you will never amount to nothing, you're stupid and will be no different than your crazy mother.' He got meaner after my grandmother died.

This uncle tormented us every chance he got. If asked whether I have ever seen hate from someone, I will point to him because he enjoyed being mean to us. One dirty thing he did to us was to wipe his hand on his tongue and then rub it across our faces and he had horrible breath.

My grandmother got sick one year and had serious constipation.

I had the same dream twice that year when she was consistently constipated that she died. They both happened before she got diagnosed with stomach cancer. My sister overheard my good uncle one day telling my mean uncle that our grandmother has cancer and the doctor says it's really bad. When my sister told me, both of us feared what would happen should she die! She died a couple of weeks after she was admitted to the hospital. I was home when my best friend at that time called me to give me the bad news. It was the worst news any pre-teen can have, knowing that the person who protected you and loved you for all these years died and gone, never to see me graduate, have kids, or get married. I knew life would change and so it did. I mourned my grandmother for the next couple of years until I reached 17 years old. I will tell you about my teenage years in the next chapter but before you read on kindly note that every time I had a bad experience I cried for my grandmother who never came to my rescue. I could not understand why I had to experience all this pain. I always asked the question 'why me?'

3 THE TEEN AGE YEARS

I was 12 going to 13 when my grandmother died and that was when my whole life went from happy to dirt. My Grandmother left the house in our mean uncle's name because he was her youngest and he tormented us to leave daily. He outwardly asked us 'why ya'll don't leave the house and don't come back'? He would also get his friend who lived a couple of doors down to call us and tell us (me and my sister) what nasty inappropriate things he would do to us minors. The neighbor would also call us sluts and whores and how he wants to fuck us. Yes, he was a sick bastard! We were minors and this man who could be our father wanted to touch us inappropriately.

I was talking to a cousin one day because I saw her on my way home from school and she told me to come live with her and get away from my uncles. I took her up on her offer and moved into her studio apartment just me and her.

Although the apartment was a small studio, we lived comfortably together because she was like the fun big sister.

My cousin had many male friends who came over to chill and that is what they did, chill and made us laugh. They all highly respected her, and I was the one not to mess with since most of them thought I was her little sister.

Some of these guys liked my cousin so we got to go to the club free and dance with the tourist since my cousin only liked the tourist club.

Those were the days, then 6 months later since living with my cousin we had to move out because she could not afford to pay the rent anymore. My cousin moved back home with her mom and since her mom's house was so small I couldn't go there so she called my mom and I stayed the night in the house of my mom's boyfriend whom she currently lived with.

My mom called my good uncle and he got me to stay in his girlfriend's family home. This house accommodated his girlfriend and her sisters with one of my cousins who was 2 years younger than me.

I was a house girl and being a teenager all I wanted to do was talk on the phone with my friends. But there was a problem with me staying long on the phone although no one else in the house really used it. But the thing that pissed me off the most, my younger cousin was able to use the phone for as long as she wanted and it was not a problem but I guess I was not a direct family member and these were her aunties; I was only connected to my uncle's girlfriend.

I started to go out with a girl in the neighborhood that was not really my crowd, but she was the only one I knew in the neighborhood. I am so glad that I was never one of those kids that gave into peer pressure because I had a strong willpower about the things I involved myself with and I knew that I never wanted to be one of those girls whose reputation got ruined because they couldn't think for themselves but I was strong-willed and no one could influence me to do anything that I did not want to do. Thank goodness for that mentality because that kept me out of trouble with my peers along with keeping my name out of certain activities.

While I was at my uncle's girlfriend's house, my neighbor, who used to live in the same neighborhood as my grandmother came back from the USA and got in contact with me since I was like a little sister to her; therefore, whenever she came back to the island she would get in contact with me. This time, she came back because her grandfather was really ill, and she needed to put him in a senior home for old people. While she was sorting that out, one of her old school friends who lived up the road suggested that she would take care of the grandfather which means he didn't have to get admitted to a senior home and she would move in the house with the grandfather therefore, he got to stay home and have help. My neighbor agreed and asked me if I wanted to stay in the house with the lady and her kids. When that whole situation was sorted, my neighbor went back to the USA and I was living within my original neighborhood in a different house with this lady, her boys, and my neighbor's grandfather.

Everything was fine until this girl got involved with this guy that smoke drugs. He was nice at first, but when he started to sleep over, he would always find his way next to me and touch my privates while I sleep. I was in school and he was a big man. Some nights, I would wake up and pretend that I was still sleeping since I was really scared. Another thing that he also did was, when his friends came over, he would drop dirty remarks at me and treat me like shit. But he would say things that no one else would know what he is talking about while he taunted me.

I told a girlfriend about it and she told me I should tell the owner what was going on in the house. Also, around that time I had to start doing my assignments for upper school so that I could do my exams and that was when I met my best friend who became my husband. I needed to use a computer for the assignments, so I called my sister and she told me about her friend. She gave me his number and he was happy to help. I had met him a few times prior since he went to school with my sister.

He picked me up and took me to his house where he lived with his dad who was hardly in the house except for weekends.

I had everything written in my book since I never used a computer before and this was the first time I ever used a computer. He opened this blank document (Microsoft Word) on the computer and told me to write all my notes for the project. He also showed me how to use the internet to search for stuff and this was how I got the information for my school project. When I needed diagrams, he drew them for me and placed them in the document. He got involved in my project and gave me ideas and he also added them to the project.

I went by him every day and even started to sleep

over since he had 2 bedrooms for himself, so I slept in one and he slept in the other. He helped me sign up for my first email address since he realized that I did not have any and he also showed me MSN. Now if you are in your thirties or older, you will remember MSN chat and I loved it. For someone that had never used a computer, I learned the keyboard quickly and was typing away in this chat with all types of people. It was fun.

I was having so much fun in this guy's house that we became close friends. He offered me to stay with him and I could keep the room I slept in but I turned it down since I was still in school and did not want to be living with a man so early although he never did come on to me in that way. He was the first kind male, that treated me with respect.

When I decided to go back to the other house, he encouraged me to tell the owner what was going on at the house. I did and the next day she asks us both to leave the next morning.

I called my cousin that my sister used to live with and

told her I had nowhere to go, asking if I could stay by her and she did not hesitate to say 'NO'.

That day I went to school, I was scared of having to sleep on the streets, and I told my Guidance Counselor who called everyone that owned a house in my family and they all said 'no'; she even called my aunt that lives in a 3 bedroom house with only her and her son and she said 'no'.

The final call my Guidance Counselor made was to my kind uncle and he got me back to the house of his girlfriend. I knew they hated me there and did not want me in the house so that night I cried myself to sleep in silent pain of not being wanted by anyone in my family. They all liked my sister and favored her so what was wrong with me? Was I that ugly, was I that bad? Is something wrong with me that I am hated so much by my family? I pulled my own hair, hit myself on the head, and cried myself to sleep while feeling completely unwanted.

4 MY FAVORED SISTER

Here are some reasons why I say that my family favored my sister.

When my grandmother was alive, my mother as crazy as she was told me one day 'when you go by my family they might favor your sister because of her color since she is clearer than you and you are full brown skin.'

First incident:

We started to go by our aunt when I was 10/11 years old and spend the weekends. One weekend, my sister went without me and came back with a nice blue pen. I asked her where she got it and she told me 'aunty has a whole bunch of these pens, I saw them and asked her for one; so when you go up, you can ask her and I am sure she will give you.'

I went up the following weekend, and I looked where my sister told me the pens were located to make sure she still had before I asked for any. I saw a whole bunch of pens, now here I go with my fast self and asked my aunt ' aunty do you have any more of those pens you gave my sister because I love how it writes' and she responded 'no I do not have any more pens they are all gone.' I could not understand why she would lie about a pen. I walked away feeling bad and recognized at that moment my mother was right when she told me that her family would favor my sister more because of color. What was the most hurtful in this particular situation was that sometime after I had asked for the pen, my aunt could not find her pens and accused me of stealing them. Therefore, I stopped visiting her.

Second incident:

When I had nowhere else to go, I called the cousin my sister used to live with to tell her that I would like to stay with her until I find somewhere to live, she did not hesitate to tell me 'NO'!

I could list a whole lot of stuff but I won't; all I can tell you is, the favoritism was so obvious that whenever my sister and I got into an argument, she would always say 'that is why all our family loves me more than you'.

My most hurtful incident happened when the same cousin that told me 'No' about moving in with her was separated from her husband and going through her divorce, she asked me to come and help her with the kids, which I obliged. Yes, I forgave her because I never was good at holding people in my heart. The thing is she was living with the same aunt I swore never to go by again but I went because she really needed the help with the kids.

I was 18 years old living with my boyfriend and he would come for me after work to catch the bus to go home. On this particular night when my aunt came home, he was there and we left shortly after.

We went to his best friend house before going home

and while we were there, my phone rang and my cousin with the kids was calling to ask me 'hey, did you see Auntie's gold ring while you were here?' I said 'no but her house is messy, so maybe you should look through the mess on the table, and you may find it.' About 5 minutes later, my cousin called back and asked me 'hey I have not seen it, are you sure you did not see her ring' and I replied 'cuz you are behaving like I stole the ring when I do not even wear jewelry, so why would I take her ring?' My cousin said 'no I was just asking, do not worry I would go and look properly. The third time she called back and asked me 'can you think back to when you were in the house if you saw it?' I said 'do not call me and ask me about any ring anymore, I do not steal, that is not how my grandmother raised me' and I hung up on her.

I was so mad because I have been to this cousin's house in the past and she knows I have never stolen anything from her.

The next morning, my cousin calls me to tell me that

my aunt found the ring under all the junk she had on the table. She also said, 'I am so sorry about last night but it was aunty that had me calling you and she was standing there right by the phone convinced that you stole her ring. Aunty even said that you stole pens from her in the past and if she does not find her ring she will call a Sergeant friend of hers for you because you do steal, but I told her I have never had any incidents with you stealing for all the times you came by me. This broke me and I just cried I could not understand how my aunt could hate me so much to accuse me of stealing to the point where she wants to call the police for me. Since that day, I have never gone to her house again. When I see her on the streets I would say 'hi' but I call her by her first name because I lost all respect for her.

5 MOVING IN WITH DAD

Let's go back to the day I was looking for someplace to live and ended up crying myself to sleep at my uncle girlfriends house that did not want me.

In the morning, my uncle came and told me my father would take me in.

Now you might ask why I never thought of living with my dad? I didn't want to live with my dad because I knew he would let me get away with anything and I knew that would not be good because children need to have some sort of discipline.

I was 15 years when I moved into my father's house and we did not get along because I came and clean his nasty house which had a scent while his girlfriend who was

16 or 17 years complained each time. Kindly note she was slow and did not have much common sense.

Then the best part happened, after about 2 months of living with my father, the lady who I am convinced was in love with one of my uncles, who lived a couple of houses down told me to come to live with her. She lived there with her daughter, her best friend, and her best friend's daughter. She thought me how to be a lady and how to take care of myself. She made sure that I studied, and I always came home to a well-cooked meal. Those were the best days of my teenage life. I had to be in the house at a certain time, but I was allowed phone time and a warm bed to sleep in. That was 'the life' until…. I turned 17 and started working.

When I started working, from my first 2 week paycheck I gave her $100.00 out of the $500.00 that I earned and she flipped the switch and called me all kinds of names like whore and slut and I was forced to give her half my paycheck when I got paid every 2 weeks.

I ended up moving into my best friend's house when I

turned 18 years old. He was nice and well he became my husband.

6 MY BEST-FRIEND TURNED HUSBAND

While I was in school, he was the guy that helped me with my school project. Remember that story I told you when I had to do my school assignment? This is the same guy.

When I moved in with my father, we got in contact again and we use to hang out a lot. The lady I lived with used to tease me saying that my best-friend liked me and he seems like a nice guy. I confronted him about it one night on my way home, and I asked him 'do you like me? Everyone says that you like me and that is why I am asking' he said 'yes I like you' and I responded 'well I would learn to like you then because you do so much for me and we aren't in a relationship.'

I knew how it was when I lived with my best friend when I was in school; therefore, I moved in with him and we got along fine. I was happy again we lived in his stepdad's house with his sister because I was really lazy and didn't have any training with taking care of the house or man for that matter and therefore, my best friend thought me how to fold my clothes and clean the house but he was way better at this than me. He also helped me to believe in myself because every time I did something wrong, I would freak out and call myself stupid and saying things like 'I would never amount to nothing, my uncle was right'. My best friend showed me all the cool things about myself although he too had some self-confidence issues, he really did work with me to get over that hurdle of self-doubt somewhat. I was not allowed to go partying and drinking since he did not like it and I always wanted to please him since in my head I could not survive this world on my own. I stopped talking to a lot of family and friends since he did not like something about them and they were all a bad influence on me. In my head, life was good. Whenever I got paid, I gave him all the money since he was the man and if I wanted anything, I had to go to him and asked for permission. Now you might be wondering how I gave him all the money every time I got paid. Well, I got online banking at the same bank as him and he knew my bank card number; therefore, he would look and see what I got paid and say what we would spend the money for and this is how he got in charge of saying how money was to be spent since he was supposed to be the smart one out of the two of us.

He was into race cars and our money got spent on turbo and exhaust, fancy rims and since I was a complete pleaser, I always thought that I was doing the right thing with him. The thing is, I never had money to buy clothes or more than one handbag because we never had enough money to buy those things. I must say on my birthdays I would get probably that camera I wanted or that mp3 player that I looked at during the year. So I did get the big things I wanted on my birthdays in those years.

These were the good days in our relationship, we had a computer, television and a phone but now I rarely use the phone because I thought everyone was using me because they wanted something granted; it seemed like they did because whenever anyone that I called friend had a problem that is when they would call me for advice. So, I basically shut off myself from people and focused on pleasing my boyfriend.

Our days were spent watching television, playing video games on the Xbox, and talking about his car and turbocharging it. When his car was turbocharged, it had to get rims because it had to look cool. I went everywhere with him although I got bored listening to all the car talk but after a while I stopped going with him because I am a big child when I get bored but it never seemed to matter when I got bored because, despite the fact that I got bored, he would still stay and talk. When it came to me talking with someone and he got bored, he would signal to me that he was ready and being an obedient girlfriend, I would say my goodbyes.

My boyfriend decided that I should get my driver's license so I could drive his car. So, I went to manual driving lessons every Sunday and I got my actual license in June 2007. The thing is I was so insecure that I was scared to drive on the road on my own because I thought all these bad things would happen. So I did not drive my boyfriend's race car because I was scared of everything.

In 2007, my father died of a diabetic stroke, and around that time he was home from work, my boyfriend did not attend the funeral with me because he hated funerals. I was in contact with my first boyfriend who gave me a drop home from the funeral. My best friend (boyfriend) and I knew I was still in love with him, after all, the first boyfriend's love is always hard to let go of, especially when they are the first one to every show you love and care. So, with all my insecurities I slept with him and I also kissed this guy I used to flirt with when I was in school. My best friend (boyfriend) found out and that made me send them both a message that I would not speak to either of them again.

7 MARRIED LIFE

The following year, we got engaged on New Year's and got married 9 months later. I was super happy to be called someone's wife.

My life had turned into no parties not even work parties or friends and absolutely no drinking alcohol since these were things that my husband did not approve of. Therefore, I would go to work and come home. If my husband saw me getting too close to someone at work, he always had a 'be careful' excuse behind it and after years of this, I realized that it was just that he wanted me for himself. I must say he did train me to clean and how he did this was if I put something out of place let's say on the dresser in the bedroom and I am outside washing clothes or especially if I am watching TV, he would call my name in a hard rough voice and I would drop whatever I was doing and run to him, to find out I placed the cream backward when it was supposed to be forward. I used to do whatever he told me to do and if he wanted to buy something with our money, I always gave in, while if I wanted something I had to give a presentation and paint a whole picture for it.

His mother hated to see how he treated me when I went to visit her. For example, he would be sitting at the table and want something from the middle of the table and I would be in the kitchen with his mother helping her or just chatting while she cook, and he would call me to hand him what is right in front of him; all he had to do is stretch for it. She would say 'I can't believe you called her to hand you something right in front of you, do not give him that let him get it himself.' He would respond 'don't mind my mother, just remember you have to go home with me' and out of fear I would go and give him what he wanted saying 'you do get me sick'. But I thought I was in love and after all, it is said in the Bible: a wife should submit to her husband.

In 2009, we finally got our first apartment and life was perfect. It was a one-bedroom in the heights which we struggled to pay whenever I got laid off from work. But we had everything we needed to live comfortably in the apartment and my husband even changed the race car and bought a brand new Suzuki swift, so I can drive since it was an automatic transmission.

I drove sometimes but I preferred him to drive because I still had fears. At this point in my life, I still suffered from a lot of fears; therefore, my safe place was at home in front of the television watching some sort of series or movie. I got pregnant in 2010 so we took the new Suzuki swift back to the company that we bought it from so that we would be able to provide for the baby on the way. We ended up purchasing an older car but it was a Subaru since this was my husband's dream car and he said it was a strong car that would be perfect for having a baby.

8 THE MOVIE

At work, I became friends with a girl in my department, and one day she told me 'I have something to show you and it's going to blow your mind, sit here and watch this video I will watch the kids'. The movie she showed me was 'The Secret' and I was completely blown away because there were so many things in that movie that I knew I had previous experiences to prove that the Law of Attraction does work and I was hooked. It brought me back to the days when my Grandmother was alive and I used to be sick every month vomiting and weak unable to get out of bed which means I was always at the clinic getting medication for something that would happen the next month. One day my Grandmother looked at me and said, 'you can heal yourself, all you have to do is ask God to heal you and believe that you are healed'. I believed her every word and as a child, I had a very big imagination, so as I lay there in my sickbed, I imagined what my sickness looked like inside my body and I then saw myself as an adult telling someone 'I can't remember the last time I was sick like this vomiting and weak; I only experienced this when I was a child'. That was the last month as a child that I ever had that type of sickness and one day while my husband and I were living with my sister, I got sick vomiting, weak and it reminded me of being a child and I said to my husband "I can't remember the last time I was sick like this vomiting and weak; I only experienced this when I was a child' and in that moment I remembered my prayer for healing.

This video also reminded me of the times when I was a teenager, when the girls and I would talk about getting married when we got older, I would always say I'll get married at 21 years old to a tall man with good-looking hair and I certainly did get married at 21 and my husband was tall and had good-looking hair.

The one memory that really hit home for me was conceiving my daughter which was intentional for me.

Scared to be Me

9 THE MEAN BOSS: FIRST PREGNANCY

In 2010, I got pregnant and at the time where I worked, we had different shifts in a kids club which is like summer camp for the children that would stay in the hotel where I worked, with the earliest shift being 8:30 – 5 pm and the latest shift being 11:30 am – 8 pm. I was pregnant at the same time with another colleague whom the boss favored.

I want to include that mean people are just not happy in their current life situations or with themselves and that is why they are mean.

My colleague was due in July and I was due in October 2010. Our jobs included going into the swimming pool and running around. Now, as much fun as that sounds, we were looking after kids that will kick you in the water and hit at you no matter if you are pregnant or not, when they were having fun expect it to get out of hand, especially the ones that lacked a lot of attention from their parents.

My boss started to put me on all the late shifts and put the other girl who was also pregnant on all the early shifts. When I inquired as to why I was being left at night alone with about 15-20 kids on my own being 5 months pregnant, with swollen feet, and hardly able to climb the stairs, I was told the other girl has to get home to her family. What my boss did not know was the other 2 workers that were not pregnant exchanged shifts with me sometimes and allowed me to go home early and I will always be grateful to them.

The other thing my boss did was, she planned a surprised baby shower for the other girl only and got all the babysitters to give her presents for her baby. The thing is my same boss also asked the girl that was my friend 'do you think that Beth would be jealous that I gave Julie a baby shower and not her?'

My boss made sure that I was there for the baby shower as she scheduled me to work on that day. But my friend pulled me aside and warned me to hide my feelings as much as I can because the bitch is looking for me to be sad and feel bad because they are all celebrating the other girl's baby.

A month before my daughter was born, I had a dream that my husband died and it was so real that I was crying my eyes out in my sleep and I woke up to my husband telling me 'wake up, wake up, it's only a dream, you are having a nightmare.' When he asked me what I was dreaming about, I told him 'I dreamt that you died'. What had me at ease about the dream is anytime I had dreamt someone died, they would die once I dream it more than once. But I dreamt this once, so I did not worry only felt weird

To sidetrack a bit, the same year my grandmother

died, I had the same dream twice that she died. In September of the same year, she died.

Now back to the baby. On October 3rd, 2010, I was sent to the hospital by the private doctor because my blood pressure was too high, and although the doctors broke my water the baby would not come, so I was rushed into surgery to have a caesarian section. I did not fall asleep while in surgery so when my baby girl was born the doctor brought her over and my newborn baby turned her head away from the doctor and looked me directly in the eyes when the doctor said 'you have a healthy baby girl'. I was sent to the recovery room where they wait until all the numbness has gone from the injections before they take you to the ward with all the other mothers. While I was in recovery, my husband came in and ask me how much longer I would be in there because our daughter was taken to the ICU (Intensive Care Unit) so I forced myself to feel and fight the medication so that I could get out of recovery and see my child.

I came out too late that night and had to wait until the

next day. The Pediatrician who was the doctor for my daughter came to my hospital bed in the morning and told me that they don't know what happen and are still trying to figure out how my healthy baby has taken a turn for the worst and she might not make it until the next day. My husband visited me in the hospital and we both went to the ICU (Intensive Care Unit) to see her. Our daughter was hooked up to all these machines it was so painful to watch but we talked to her and prayed that she would be ok.

I was woken up at about 2 a.m., I was asked to go to the ICU because they said my daughter would not make it through the night so I called my husband who did not want me to go visit her without him and as the obedient wife I waited until he drove there and then we both went down to the ICU. We got to see her, and then they asked us to go into the waiting room while we were in there, we heard the machine beeping and saw the nurses all around her little case that she was in, with one nurse making sure we don't come out the room as they tried to revive her. My baby was gone and I was in disbelief I did not have the luxury of breaking down and crying since I was there trying to calm down my husband from throwing the hospital furniture around. It was all about calming him down so what I did is suppressed the hurt as much as I could and today as I write my story is the first day I really cried about the situation.

After they cleaned her up and wrapped her, we were allowed to go in and see her and hold her and that was the first and only time I have ever seen 'peace', yes my baby was gone but she looked like 'peace' that's the only way I can describe it.

Since I lost my baby, I was required to return to work sooner since I was not allowed maternity leave. My workplace gave me 6 weeks off to heal and on the week that I was to return my boss called and asked me 'would you be jealous when you come back out to work because everyone has their children and you don't have your own?' How inconsiderate I know but she was a lost BITCH who I replied 'I would not be jealous of other people and their children because they are not mine and I do not long for stuff that don't belong to me'. My boss did not send Human Resources an email to update about my baby dying which our Human Resources would have sent an email out to every department notifying them about the loss of my baby and it would have been easy not to have to answer the question 'how is the baby'. So when I return to work and people were asking 'how is the baby' I had to re-live the event and tell them 'my baby died there is no baby'. The other thing is when I returned to work, I could not be caught feeling sad about losing my baby in public because my boss was the type of person who feasts on other people's failures and from what I understand she was happy that I lost my child.

My friend at the time who worked in the same department told me 'girl if there is one thing you don't do is give her the joy of seeing you sad or crying so if you ever feel sad and want to cry let me know and I'll watch the kids while you go to the bathroom. She was a very good friend and I did have a couple of those moments and she would watch the children while I go and have my moment but the thing is I never cried with tears but I had this big sadness within. I must say with a past that I had as a child I had become brilliant with suppressing my feelings. So I faked a smile every day until it became a real smile. There were the times I caught my boss steering at me since all I did was smile. In December of that year, my boss who did not usually leave her office, went down to Human Resources to collect the gifts from the hotel for the staff who has kids and when she came back up I was in the office, and as she took out each gift she made sure she said 'this is for Keith child, and this is for Mary's child' until she took all the gifts out and at the end, she said 'and that's all the gifts for their children'. But I refused to show any sadness or to react in any way to give her any satisfaction of feeling good off my mourning.

10 SECOND PREGNANCY

In 2011, my work colleague went away to the USA and brought me a pack of 24 pregnancy tests because I asked her to since I had actively started back trying to get pregnant and every time I thought I was pregnant it would come out negative. I have never felt so miserable and non-deserving in my life. Here I was young, married, living with my husband and all pink baby playpen, pink high chair, pink car seat and pink stroller along with a drawer full of baby girl onesies, socks, wash clothes, cute sandals and no month would any of those 24 pregnancy tests say positive and I was convinced something was wrong with me. I started to lose hope of ever getting pregnant again. My husband was not one to really have that heart to heart, so I bore these feelings on my own and he did his on his own. Plus he was never a person to want to seek help for something like this so it was natural pregnancy or no pregnancy.

In March 2012, I attended a close friend baby shower who was pregnant with her second child. She became friends with me after I lost my child because she had experience losing a child and wanted to help me get through it. So here I was, trying to stay happy at this party but all I could think of was 'how is it that she's on her second child and God you can't even give me one'? I tried my best to smile and play the games but she saw through me and a couple of days after the party, she called me and we talked about it. My girlfriend understood my feelings as she was there when she wanted her first pregnancy and she told me to talk to God about it.

So after our phone call, I found myself a quiet place and this is the conversation I had with God: 'Hi, I am here to have this conversation with you about what I really want when it comes to getting my baby. I want a girl child and I want her to be born in the month of December since that is my birth month. I want my daughter to have good-looking hair like my husband because I cannot plait hair and therefore, she cannot have my thick hair. I want her to have my husband's eyes and she would have a perfect blend of facial looks between the 2 of us. For me to have a baby in December I would have to get pregnant in April, so if I don't get pregnant next month April, give me the strength to wait until the next year 2013 April. This is the last time I would have this conversation and help me not to worry going forward.

At the end of March, my husband agreed to pay for this ovulation app I had on my iPhone at the time. This app I have been using since January 2012 and I had to put my period dates as this app was supposed to assist people like me who have irregular periods but I was using the free app this whole time. Coming to the end of March after my period had finished for the month, my husband agreed to pay for the pregnancy app for the month of April.

On April 2nd, 2012, the deed was done, and the app was telling me to take a pregnancy test at the end of the next week. I followed the instructions, and we brought the pregnancy test as instructed.

I got up early the next morning to take the test. I went to the bathroom with the test, took it out of the package, and when it was time to pee nothing came, I was so nervous that when I forced it I got 2 drops only, so I placed it on the floor and finished pee giving it the few minutes it needed to read. While the test lay on the floor in front of the toilet, I only saw one line show up and the second line did not show. In disappointment, I said 'well this means I've got to wait until next year April so give me the strength'.

As I proceeded to take the test off the floor, I saw something like a faded line so I put the test right In front of my left eye to make sure that I was seeing correctly. 'YESSSSSS' I am finally pregnant' I screamed in my head. I got off the toilet so fast wash my hands and bolted to the bedroom to wake up my husband. He was not happy I woke him up from his sleep but when he caught himself and I said I have something to show you, his face lit up because I was finally pregnant again.

We made an appointment with the same doctor we were referred to with our first baby since he was a top doctor in our country to confirm the pregnancy and it was true I was pregnant, due to deliver December 24th, 2012.

The plan with the pregnancy was to go to a private doctor until the final month and then get transferred to the hospital so we don't have to pay for delivery since health care in our country is free at our public hospital. When I was 5 months pregnant, at one of our doctor's visits, I asked the doctor about the cost to schedule a C-Section as this was the way I wanted to have my baby. He told me that to have a scheduled C-Section I would have to pay $3000.00-$4000.00 between paying him and the hospital for the surgery. When I heard this price, I told my husband 'we are not paying that money and if we are supposed to have a C-

Section, God will provide a way'.

This prompted me to go and have another conversation with God. I found myself a quiet place and I said 'I want to have a C-Section scheduled but I am not paying for it. Also, I want my baby to be born on the 20th December because I cannot handle being at work in all that Christmas hassle, especially knowing how my boss is and how she treated me in my last pregnancy.

What is the Christmas hassle?

On Christmas Eve each year, the hotel where I worked gave gifts to all the guests staying in the hotel, so since we were in the kids' department, we were in charge of getting all the children gifts in bags with their individual names on a gift bag which was presented to them by the Elves on Christmas Eve. For the kids that did not show up to receive their gifts, we had to take the gifts to them to their individual rooms with the Elves to present them at the door. I was the person in charge each year to get these gifts ready and make sure that every gift is accounted for and each child receives gifts. Each year, I created a list of names of the children who would be staying in the hotel along with the owners' kids list, wrote the tags and I always escorted the gifts to the relevant rooms with Elves which I use to enjoy. I did not want to do that this year and I know how mean my boss is, therefore, once my baby came on 20th December, I would not be at work and she would have to find someone else to do that. I remember how swollen I was the last time I was approaching 40 weeks so there was no way I would be able to handle going up all those stairs and running around the hotel to these different rooms.

My Pregnancy Story Continues:

When I was 8 months pregnant, I had to get a blood test which indicated that my blood sugar was high and I had to go on a special diet, otherwise I would end up with diabetes, then I would have to go on insulin, which I did not want because I hate the idea of taking medication while being pregnant.

I did really well with keeping within my eating parameters but with all the stress at work that I was having from my boss again my husband started to panic saying 'we might lose this baby again because everything seems to be going wrong, you are on a special diet, your boss is still giving you extra stress and with this pregnancy, you have been so sick.' I told him 'this is how I know that this baby will be born healthy and we will finally have a little girl because everything is going wrong so that means that when she is born everything will be perfect.' He looked at me in disbelief because I was the one that was experiencing all these things directly and he could not understand why I was so calm and sure, but I knew how everything happened, I knew how I prayed and I even remembered the day I conceived April 2nd and in that moment I recognized that I will have a healthy baby girl, therefore, I was opened to the fact that if I had to give birth to my daughter naturally that God would give me the strength to push and if I had to work on Christmas Eve I would be able to manage. So, while my husband worried about my entire pregnancy which if I was not as sure as I was in what I was attracting, he would have had me in that negative thinking. But since I was seeing everything I asked for unfolding as I had requested with the pregnancy so far and the knowledge that once I believe and leave it knowing that it will happen I knew my baby girl will be in that car seat driving in the back of the car and I'm looking across at my husband saying 'you could imagine we are actually parents'?

We visited the private doctor until I turned 36 / 37 weeks, then he gave us a letter to take to the public hospital where I was supposed to go for the next 3 visits until my due date.

On our first visit to the hospital, my husband said to me 'I am not really looking to come back here every week because I know we will be here all day'. I told him 'if that is what you want, you should ask God for it.' We did stay the whole morning waiting to see the doctor but when we got into the doctor's office guess who was my doctor, the one and only MY PRIVATE DOCTOR was seeing me for free at the hospital. Now, you might ask why this is a shock? The way that hospital works, you go to the front desk and they give you a date to come and see the hospital doctor which is available and the doctors change every day so certain doctors come on certain days. So, when I saw that my private doctor was the doctor, I was so shocked because this was not humanly planned.

The Private Doctor told me to get on the examiner's table so he can check the baby and see how the baby was doing, he also asked me permission for his trainee doctors to come into the room and I said 'sure'. After the examination, he left me so that I could put my clothes back on. I went outside to talk to him as he always did after he examined me.

I sat in the chair next to his table, my husband stood behind me and his trainee doctors all stood in a row against the wall next to him. The doctor said 'Mrs. Parris, all that time you visited me privately I did not realize what happened to you the last time with losing your baby therefore, I have spoken to the team and we have decided to schedule you a C-section for next week Thursday.' I nearly jumped out of my seat with excitement and one of the trainee doctors looked across at me and said 'I have never seen anyone get excited to receive a C-section you are a first.' I smiled and asked the question out loud 'what date is next week Thursday?' The Doctor replied 'next Thursday is the 20th December 'I was so excited and overjoyed and they all looked at me so strange probably saying 'that lady is crazy' they all laughed at my excitement as I was leaving while my husband was freaking out as we walked back to the car.

On December 20th, 2012, my daughter was born — she had beautiful green eyes and she was sleeping on a side since she was born.

We left the hospital on December 24th, 2012, and I became a single mom who was married for the next couple of years.

11 MARRIED SINGLE MOM

The first week my daughter came home, my husband cleaned her diaper once and then told me 'this is nasty and you should be the one to always clean her since she is a girl and I feel funny touching her vagina'. I understood what he was saying but I never thought he meant never. Since that day my husband made sure to call me whenever our daughter had to go to the toilet to clean her. I changed all her pampers and I also was the one to always clean her when she started to use the toilet until I moved out.

I was not only required to clean my daughter but also to feed her and bathe her, but he did not want me to discipline her.

An example of this is, my husband would be in the bedroom and my daughter would be on the toilet, even though I am cooking, he would call me to come and clean her because 'you know this is not my thing' he would say.

He would be in the kitchen, and our daughter would want some food, and he would go to the fridge, get something out of the fridge, and still expect me to come and get the food for her because 'I did not know how much food to put out' was another excuse.

Whenever it was time for her to go to sleep, he would say 'you know this is your expertise' which made me get in the habit of falling to sleep at 8:30 pm every night since that was the time she would fall asleep.

I used to fret at times, especially if I am cooking and have to stop to go and do something for our daughter and he is just sitting there doing nothing but waiting for food and no matter how much I fret, he would not pay me any attention because he used to call me miserable and lazy or use the excuse of 'you are her mother and normally the woman do these things. He never looked at it from the point that I had to stop in the middle of cleaning the kitchen or waiting for his lasagna to bake to come and do something he was capable of doing for our daughter. I was truly a married single mother.

12 *STARTED EXERCISING*

When our daughter was 2 years old, I was at work one day and I left my department to go to another department to collect something and while I was there, a guy saw me and said 'Beth you are getting bigger and bigger so you are nearly fat but you aren't there yet' all I heard was 'you are getting fat' and at that moment I made a mental conscious decision to watch how much I was eating and to look into losing weight. I was 5'1 and 136 pounds but I looked chubby; my butt and stomach were competing with each other. When I got back to my department that same day I said to everyone 'I am going to cut back on my eating so I will eat smaller portions, this is not a diet I am just teaching myself how to not eat so much' one girl laughed at me and said 'you could never eat less, you love your stomach and food too much' this was the comment that confirmed my way of eating because I was going to prove everyone wrong.

When I got my lunch from work each day, I would cut the food in half so for example if I got rice and chicken and the chicken piece was a leg and thigh, I would half the rice and separate the leg from the thigh and eat the half portion of rice and the leg. Then for dinner, I would eat the other half of the rice and the thigh. I ate like this from April to September and dropped off a few pounds. The thing is that by September I was only eating lunch but not dinner because the half at lunch was making me full completely; so when dinner time came, I was not hungry, which I thought was amazing because I am never one to stay hungry or starve myself.

In late August, I saw a friend that I went to school with who was super fit start her exercising program up again and it was at a reasonable price which I could afford. I told my husband about me going to exercise to tone my body and he said 'who tell you that I want you to exercise; I am fine with how you are' and I replied with annoyance 'everything I do does not always revolve around you'! He was so mad at that statement that he stormed out of the room. This was the very first time I was going to do something that he did not agree on. But this was also the first time in our relationship that I stuck to doing something that he did not want me to do.

My exercise classes were on Mondays, Tuesdays, and Thursdays for an hour each session, and every time I left for class my husband would push our 2-year-old daughter at me telling her to 'go to your mother' especially when I was getting ready should she want something. Then when I would be getting ready to go through the door, he would tell her mommy is leaving and she would come running to me screaming crying for me not to leave and he would just sit there not helping to get her off me. I kept strong in these situations and I would look my daughter in the eyes and say 'daddy is here and mommy is coming back'. I would go to the door and tell her 'mommy has to go', which was painful as a mother we never want our children to cry but I was not letting my husband win and not get myself in shape. There were many times I would drive off watching my daughter in the rearview mirror balling her eyes out and daddy would be inside making sure not to come and calm her down until I was completely gone.

When the exercise program was over, I was 120 pounds and my body was fit and tone which made me want to start all over again, but this time, my husband won by telling me 'I do not mind you exercising but it is really hard on our daughter when you go out like that, so it might be best for you to stop and wait until she is older'. This is when I picked up running in our area early in the morning to maintain my body and keeping myself fit because I did not want to go back to that unhealthy body that I had before the program. I fell in love with running and did it for 2 years keeping my body looking nice and fit along with eating healthier so I could maintain my weight.

In my first year of running, my husband did not mind because I ran in the area where we lived and he would know when I leave home and be able to time when I would get back.

The second year, we moved from where we lived and I needed to find someplace to go running where I felt safe because our new area had lots of dogs; therefore, there was no way I would run out there. I started to go to our local board-walk but it started to get creepy each time I went and some guy would come and try talking up to me, he even stopped running and would just stand and watch me, so I decided to switch locations deciding to go running by our work since it was a long road with no dogs, no one to talk up to me and the road is always busy with workers driving pass; I knew I would feel safe there.

The first time I went running was when I was going to the park at the bottom of the hill where my husband worked and run up the hill. But that morning I had to go to another department to pick up money for an administrative job I did and at that moment I decided to park at the top of the hill where I would be forced to run back up because I know I would start out running downhill and to get to my car I would have to run back up. This was a task and I struggled to get uphill without stopping but over time I achieved it, so I pushed myself to run faster. After my run, I would stay and talk to the workers to give my body time to cool down and muscles to relax before I got in my car to drive home. My husband hated this and at first, he would ask if I could not go running anywhere else because he did not like it because the location was too far. I said 'no I feel comfortable and I am getting to challenge myself each time', so what he started to do is first say 'when you go running and I have to go to work who is going to keep our daughter' I said 'but you do not work on Saturdays' well guess what, he started to work on Saturdays but the thing is his sisters lived with us at the time and his mother lived down the road from us. He used to go to his mom before work in the morning sometimes to collect eggs since her husband sold eggs and my husband would advertise and get them sales. I told my husband 'take our daughter to your mother, she said it is ok, and I would pick her up from there when I get home' he said 'ok' but when the Saturday came he would call me and say I have our daughter you can come and pick her up from the office when you are finished'. He even refused to leave her with his sisters and when he did, he would then send a message saying that they are going out and I have to come home soon.

My husband did not like me hanging out with anyone he did not know, he did not like me to have friends and he did not like to be left with our daughter to do anything because he was not good and I was the best person to do her tea, her cereal, her everything. This was his way of keeping me on a tight leech which made me feel like I was suffocating most days. I continued my running and stood up for myself when it came to exercising.

13 *THE PARTIES*

The year I started to exercise, I did Rhonda Byrne's 28-day gratitude exercises from her book 'The Magic' with 4 women on my WhatsApp that I put together which was a friend from work, a lady I met online, my daughter's nursery teacher, and myself. We all did these to attract something in our lives and I really wanted to attract my own car which I did. My husband finally agreed to get me my own car which is what I had used to go to all those exercise classes and my goal was to fit into a size small dress by December because that is when our staff party took place.

I knew I could not ask my husband to buy a dress for

the staff party because he would tell me 'no we don't have any money or I do not want you to go to that type of party' therefore I message my cousin who lives in Canada who is like a sister to me asking her for the dress and she opted to buy me shoes, bag and earrings.

This would be the first party I went to in years since my husband did not like me going to parties, I had stopped but after doing the exercising and realizing when I do what I want I am actually happy. I was adamant that no matter what I was going to this staff party. Now I had to get money to do my hair and nails so I told my husband in November that when the staff party comes around I am going this time since I have never been, he was not happy and said but I never went and it's not a big thing. I said to him 'all I want is to get my hair and nails done because my cousin is buying me the dress.' When the time came around for the party, I made sure to take the money out of my account as soon as I got paid because I know that when my husband gets a hold of the money he would make use of it so that I couldn't go. He made mention that he is not going and I told him but he could come and he said 'the only reason I would go to that party is to watch you all night making sure no one dances with you'. I told him 'well you stay home I do not need a bodyguard because that would be uncomfortable plus I naturally do not like people dancing on me when I go out'.

I got my sister to do my makeup and I went to the party and I had the time of my life! I had so much fun that I remembered how much I love dancing and music. I do not drink since I dropped that when I and my husband were boyfriend and girlfriend because he did not drink, and he did not want me to drink. I only used to drink at home because I never trust drinking when I was out since I never wanted to ever be one of those ladies who people put something in their drink plus drinking used to make me sleepy and tired. But since he did not want me to drink, I did not buy alcohol for home.

In December of the same year that I went to the Christmas party, I won the star of the month award at work which means I would receive an award in March when we have our staff awards show.

Since the staff party, my husband did not want me to go to parties anymore, he would like me to just stay like I used to be before. How do I know this? He started to drop comments like 'people are talking and not in a good way on how you dance at the party' I told him 'I went, I had fun, and I did not do anything inappropriate, so people would talk, they have a mouth to voice their opinion'. That was me saying I am still going to these staff parties and I am not stopping for anyone, knowing that he will come with an excuse as to why I should stay at home.

As March approached for the award show, my husband made it clear that we do not have any money to be buying anything extra, so if I wanted to go to the staff appreciation party, I would have to wear something that I own, knowing I did not have any clothes appropriate for the awards since I did not go out and was always home, my wardrobe contains jeans, tops, and church dresses.

By this time, I had made friends with a babysitter at work and she used to help me out with my daughter by taking her to school and picking her up using my car. I was not able to pay her as per my husband; therefore, I would let her use my car not worrying about gas since she was babysitting for free.

One morning, Sarah came to me with her friend; she was now dating. When she walked through the house, I was in the shower and had left the kitchen door open, she shouted, 'Beth! How is it that you told me you could not buy a $100.00 dress to go and get your award, but your husband has $2000.00 rims sitting in your kitchen? We are getting you a dress even if I have to be the person to call your husband and harass him.' When she said that I got an idea and realized that my husband loves to look like the good husband who would use our money to buy me anything because he had an image to live up to therefore, I told her 'that is exactly what we would do. We are going to go into town and when we get in a store you can call him while pretending I do not know that you are calling him, then you will tell him you know I said I cannot buy a dress but you know that he would and I am certain he will not give you any hassle, so we would be able to buy anything.'

Just as planned, we did exactly that, she waited until we were in the store, called him and said 'Hey I am in the store with Beth in town and I saw a dress that would look really nice for her to receive her award but she does not know that I called you because I wanted to ask before I told her.' He replied, 'yes you can let her use the card she has on her and it does not matter the cost just buy it'.

When my friend came off the phone, she was amazed at the completely different person he was with her saying 'wow if I did not know any different, I would say you've got a brilliant husband but how did you know that would have worked?' I replied 'I know he is big on his image and he loves to portray a good husband who cares for his wife in public. Anyway, let us get to shopping.'

I got a beautiful long gold dress, and I wore shoes, a

bag that I had at home. What my friend did was to make sure that he agreed to pay for my hair and nails to get done so that night I got my little sister to do my makeup and when I got dressed and was about to go through the door I saw my husband sitting in the living room with our daughter and in that moment I foolishly thought he would say 'honey you look beautiful' nope he just handed a very upset mad face and refused to give me a kiss before I left, so I basically had to wait until I got to the party and everyone there was amazed at how gorgeous I looked to receive my award. His excuse after this incident was 'what husband like to see his wife dress all beautiful to go out with other people and not him?' I went to the awards had a blast and came straight home. This is one of the first times in my life that I recognized that I might be beautiful.

14 PACK AND LEAVE! (1 OF 3)

This started after the awards in early April 2017. My girlfriend is the one that helped me get the dress for the awards. Sally started to date this guy and he was a good man and really romantic. Let us call him Tom. One day I was at work and my girlfriend Sally forwarded me a message that Tom sent her expressing his feelings for her and I felt the love in that message because I am that person who puts herself in the other person's shoes. Anyway, I was freaking out not only for the message but also because Sally went through a horrible breakup with another guy who broke her heart, and she was scared of commitment. Now here comes Tom serious about commitment so with my excitement I rushed to the exit of my department to go outside to call her and talk about the message being super happy. I remember this day like yesterday because I nearly ran into the door while trying to get out with excitement. My boss was in her office and saw my excitement on my phone but I am not a talker, so she didn't ask me anything.

I called Sally and we chatted about the text and ended the conversation on a very happy note. Since the text, Sally and Tom finally became a couple, and Sally wanted me and Tom to get time to get to know each other since at the time we were the most important people in her life. I helped her get over her breakup and I was there for her to receive her true love.

One Saturday, I was home with my husband and my daughter. She was playing and my husband was watching TV and I wanted to get out of the house. I messaged Sally and told her 'hey I'm home bored and I want to do something' now you might ask why I didn't tell my husband but you have to know he's a house mouse and don't like to leave home either because of gas, don't want to drive and always want to relax at home. Anyway, Sally called me and said she was with Tom and will talk to him and maybe this could be the time for us to get to know each other. When Sally called back, she told me Tom said he would take us to a restaurant, the 3 of us 'his treat' and that they would pick me up, so all I had to do was to get dressed.

I knew my husband would have a problem with me going out because he never likes me going anywhere. After all, he always wanted me to stay home.

I decided no matter what happens I will go out because I cannot allow him to continue to keep me home. I told my husband 'I am going out with Sally and her boyfriend to get to know him since Sally keeps telling me she wants me to. Sally and Tom are picking me up and we are going to a casual restaurant.' When I told my husband this, he did not reply, so I went into the bedroom to gather my clothes to press since they were coming for me in 2 hours. My husband made his way to the bedroom and started shouting at the top of his voice 'you are at home with your family and you texted Sally and told her you are bored! You are so ungrateful because if you are bored, you can go and play with your daughter, she needs her mother but NO you want to go out with your friends! As he continued to shout, I did not reply because every time in the past he would always make me feel like I am stupid and would say 'you think you are smart but you are not smart'. As our daughter stood there he said 'you are a horrible mother and you think you are a good mother but you do not know how to be a good mother. At this point, I felt like crying my eyes out because here was yet another person in my life who was supposed to love me and I just cannot seem to get it right. Then my strong self said 'no matter what he says you are going out tonight because he is only behaving like this because you are leaving the house to go out with friends and he only wants you to stay home.

After my husband finished shouting, I walked away and went into the laundry room and cried my eyes out softly because at this point in my life I had made it a habit since my encounters with my horrible boss have taught me not to let the people that hurt me see me in pain. When I was complete with releasing the pain of his horrible words, I went and got dressed and he said to me 'if you leave, do not come back!'

I left and I had so much fun with Sally and Tom; I completely cleared my mind of what happened at home and I just enjoyed the moment of seeing 2 love birds. It was a beautiful sight to see which made my night worth it.

I went back home, and my husband did not mention it and that was left because in his mind there is always a next time and there would be another opportunity to say pack and leave.

15 PACK AND LEAVE! (2 OF 3)

I use to babysit these triplets from the time they were 11 years old until they were 16, well by the time they were 14 it was a basic 'we want Beth to hang out with us because she is so much fun while mom and dad go to dinner. These kids love and trust me so much that they would tell me all their secrets and ask for advice on their teenage problems and fears. They have me as a part of their family and they always brought my daughter whatever she wanted when they were traveling to my island.

The triplets and I made a pack that when they reach age 17 we will go to the teenage night club on the island together and have some fun, so I never thought that going to a tourist night club would be a problem.

The triplets were so excited to be going out of the hotel with people other than their parents; they invited all the babysitters who swore that they were coming including me.

When I picked my daughter up from her new babysitter (not Sally but my husband's aunt), she had a cough, but I got her to sleep. At that time it seemed like she was catching a cold but I thought she would be home with daddy so she would be good and it's not like I am sleeping out, I will be back and it's only a cough.

I called my husband who was driving on the way home and told him 'our daughter has a cough but she would be fine. I am going out with the triplets tonight as I told you before; it was previously planned.' He replied, 'why are you going out when our daughter is sick?!' I said, 'it's only a cough and she would be fine plus I know that one of the triplets would not have any fun because of her insecurities around people and it is only one night.' My husband replied with his shouting voice 'you go to the club but when you leave the house, do not come back, you can pack and leave!' then he hung up on me.

I was hurt that this would be the second time my husband told me to pack and leave because this really hurt a lot, so I decided to talk to my husband about this statement by letting him know that it's not cool and it hurts, so I would like him to stop saying this to me.

When he arrived home, I said to him, "I do not want to argue with you, and you know I do not respond to your negativity when you get angry and shout, so I am hoping to have a conversation with you. He was open to this and ready to talk. I said 'why are you so against me going to this club with the triplets, after all, I told you about this last year that this year we are going to the tourist club and do not say anything about our daughter being sick because she only has a cough and she would be ok in a few hours. He replied, 'to be honest, I just do not want my wife to go to clubs where there are drinking and smoking plus they are dangerous, so I would rather you do not go. Plus I feel as if you are using the triplets as an excuse to get to go to a night club. I replied 'I am not using them to go but I know if I do not go, the youngest will be crushed plus I promised her I was coming and also you need to stop this thing where when you get vex you tell me to PACK AND LEAVE! This statement hurts' at this point a tear came down my cheek as I was truly speaking from the heart, so I allowed the pain to show. I continued 'If you do not stop saying that, there might be a day when I do pack and leave.

He replied 'ok I will not say that anymore but I still do not want my wife in any night club, so let them know you are not coming. I said ok if that makes you happy and I canceled. I sent a text message and told everyone that my daughter was sick; therefore, I was unable to attend.

When I got to work the next day, all the babysitters said when I did not come to the club, the youngest triplet stayed in a corner all night and did nothing because I did not attend.

At this point, my inner voice said 'you need to stop doing everything to please your husband because you are hurting people in the process. You always live your life to please him and end up unhappy or hurting someone else because she did not deserve this at all. I had a talk with her and she told me how hurt she was that I promised her I was coming and did not show up, but she would not hold it against me because it was for my daughter, she just wanted me to know it was not fun because I was not there.

16 PACK AND LEAVE! 3 OF 3

This 3rd pack and leave is the one that I would never forget. It was in January 2018 and I was at home with my daughter and my husband's 2 nephews aged 13 and 8 at the time. The were big boys in the living room playing video games and I was in the bedroom relaxing while my daughter was playing with her toys. There was this guy who was supposed to come to our home and look at our refrigerator and he took over 2 hours to get to our house. While waiting for this guy to arrive, I lay in my bed, and I fell asleep. About 10 minutes into my sleep, I jumped up to check on my daughter but when I opened my eyes, she was on the bed sleeping beside me. I guess she got tired and came to lie down for a nap is what I thought to myself. I told myself, the boys outside will come and get me if they hear anyone at the door, but that was not the case — the guy came and did not hear anyone because they were caught up playing video games, so they did not move. I got woken up by the sound of my husband shouting my name asking where is our daughter, he shouted with rage 'BETH, BETH, WHERE IS SANDY'! I jumped out of my bed heart-racing and husband shouting 'THE MAN CAME HERE TO FIX THE FRIDGE AND YOU WERE SLEEPING, THE FRONT DOOR WAS OPEN AND SANDY IS NOT HERE. SO SHE HAD PROBABLY GONE OUT THE DOOR. YOU ARE SUCH A HORRIBLE MOTHER! My heart continued racing as I caught myself being jumped out of my sleep with his shouting which is something I have told him for years he should not do because it's not good to be jumped out of your sleep like that but when he's angry you've got to pay.

I got up scared because not only was he shouting and

talking down to me but also my brain started to question: is it true that I am really a bad mother, after all, here I am sleeping and he's implying that she walked away which does not sound like something Sandy would do because she does not like to go anywhere unless she has either mommy or daddy and she's 5 and has never walked away before, so I started to think, I remember she was in the bed with me sleeping and the norm was for her to hide whenever daddy car pulls up so that he can find her. I paused and said to him, 'you come home, jump me out my sleep shouting and I bet Sandy is hiding in the bathroom.' I went into the bedroom which is where we both were sleeping, opened the bathroom door, and there she was hiding with the 'feeling bad look on her face' since she would have heard daddy shouting at me. Now, you might think this is the point where my husband would apologize but no he had to continue because I was so wrong to fall asleep when the guy was coming to fix the fridge which the boys outside did not come and tell me someone was outside. So as my husband carried on to calling me names along with telling me and stressing on how much of a bad mother I am, I picked up my cell phone, left him arguing with himself in the bedroom and I went into the living room to get away from his negativity and listening to him bringing me down with his most hurtful words. I blanked him out and scrolled through my phone until he came and started shouting at me 'YOU COME, COME'! I followed him although my name isn't 'you' I did not want to add fuel to the fire he was in so I did not say anything I just walked behind him. When he got to our bedroom door, he reached up high on top of our dresser, dragged down my suitcase, slammed it in front of me, and shouted with all his might 'PACK AND LEAVE'! My heart melted and I felt this is it I am tired of him telling me this and how he did this one was very degrading, so I walked straight over to the laptop and started looking for apartments, yes, I was completely tired at this point of the treats from him telling me to leave all because he thought I would be begging him to stay since I don't have any family to call on for help being the black sheep of the family and my sister the favorite. I decided I did not know how I would make it but I was leaving this time for sure and so that I don't cause any problems with him I will leave our daughter in his care because I will still get to see her.

That night, we had to leave home to pick something up and I drove my car while he sits in the back with Sandy. My husband asks' I saw you were looking at apartments on the computer, are you planning to move out?' I replied 'you told me today to pack and leave so that's what I plan to do' he said 'I did not mean that when I said it' I replied 'there are so many times you can tell someone to leave and believe there will be a day they will and that's what I planned to do.' He wanted to get annoyed but at this point, he recognized that he was treading on thin ice. But I stood my ground because at this point I had enough of his threats and unconsciously I mentally left the relationship. My husband then asks 'why don't you go to someone and stay with them and let us work this out'. I replied 'I am not going to anyone because that means I would have to be explaining what happened and I do not want anyone in my business. Plus you know I don't have a family member that I can go to that will take me in.

This put a wedge between us and now my husband was trying to see if he can fix what he had broken.

He was uncertain about if I would move since he had never seen me react this way and was shocked by my reaction too but I guess 'it is so much that a person can take' is a true statement.

My husband called me one day and suggested that we start celebrating each other's birthdays and I replied 'I find this so convenient since my birthday recently passed and yours is 4 months away, his excuse was 'we are only now going to try and fix our relationship. I agreed with the idea because he had a point.

On Valentine's Day, he got my vision board done over from pictures stuck to a bristle board with glue to a beautiful photo frame but I was missing some photos from my original vision board and he added new ones. I did not fret, instead I was grateful for the gesture but did not get him anything because this would be the first time we would celebrate Valentine's Day because my husband made it clear that he did not like that day; therefore, we never celebrated it but in my head, he was trying.

17 NO BIRTHDAY GIFT

My husband was in control of all our money, yes including mine which I had stated previously; therefore, if I wanted to buy anything even for him, I had to ask him for the money which I did after Valentine's day in late February, early March I told my husband for his birthday gift I will need $1000.00 which I secretly had planned to buy him an expensive wristwatch and then use the rest of the money to take him to dinner making our night romantic and beautiful. Please keep in mind that his birthday is in April and the work awards are in March which I had started going to every year.

As the work awards were getting close, I reminded my husband about the event and told him that this year I will wear clothes that I already have in my closet along with the shoes I own but I will pay to get my hair, nails, and makeup done which will cut my normal budget for the event by a lot.

The week before the awards, when I got paid, I took my card, went straight to the bank, and took off the money that I needed to get ready for the awards because knowing my husband he would find something to do with it and then look at me and say 'we don't have the money' as he did in the past.

The next day as he was bathing and I was calculating our weekly expenses, I recognized that we didn't have the money to pay the babysitter, so we would have to touch our joint savings account which is normal when we run low knowing it will build up because we have money automatically going there each week. Kindly note we have gone to get money from this account for his race car parts and turbos.

As he was bathing, I raised my voice so he could hear 'we have all the money for everything except the babysitter' he replied 'didn't you get paid?' I said 'yes but remember I am going to the awards, so I put aside the money for that and the remaining is not enough. But don't we have money in the credit union; we haven't gone there in a while and it's just one week' he replied with an annoyance in his voice 'use your money from the credit union but don't touch mine'! This hurt, the reason being that this is a man that whatever he wanted to make his car faster, I agreed with MY money. When he bought his $2000.00 rims and came home and told me, I did not make a fuss, I was cool and ok with whatever made him happy. I never behave like this and I hardly ask for stuff for myself. When he replied that was the final straw for me and I decided there and then that I was going to separate our money and do my finances because I always have a problem when I wanted to go anywhere and I got tired of begging to spend the money that I work hard for each week.

I didn't reply or tell him my plan because I know that in

the past he talked me out of being in control of my own money because, according to him 'I won't be able to handle it and I don't know the things he does with juggling our money plus we are a couple and our finances are better together'.

That morning we were getting ready to go to the same credit union to take off money to buy our daughter an iPad.

When we got to the credit union, I went to the counter on my own since he wanted to stay with our daughter and I am the one who's, as he puts it, 'is better talking with people'.

I went to the bank teller and drew off the money for our daughter's iPad and the babysitter. When I received it, I asked the teller 'how can I stop my money from going into the joint account? She told me, I needed to go to the desk behind me and the gentleman will help. I went to the gentleman and stopped my money from going into the joint account. When I was through and signaled my husband that I was through, he asked me why I had to go over to the desk behind me. I told him 'I stopped my money from going into the joint account' he replied 'oh why'? I said 'after this morning conversation, I decided to start being in control of my money'. We were in public, so I figured that's why he didn't react with shouting but to my surprise, he just asked a question which was: if I wanted to keep the credit card that we shared which was in his name and I replied ' no I don't. I told him I would get our bank statements and see how much money each of us put in the joint account so we can take what's ours. Knowing that most of my money went into the joint account, he suggested that we split the $2000.00 in half where I would get $1000.00 and he would get $1000.00. I agreed and said well I will use the $1000.00 for your birthday gift.

3 days later, he took me to work with my car since his car was at the mechanic and he was off and came back and picked me up when my shift was over.

On our way home, he told me 'I went to the credit union today and took out all the money from the joint account. I paid the mechanic $1500.00 and the mechanic told me that I didn't have to pay him all the money at once if I was sure but I decided to just get the expense out the way. I know you said that you don't want the credit card so the $500.00 I have left I will put as your half to pay off the credit card your part. Then that means I only owe you $500.00.'

At this moment, I remembered his gift for next month and told myself although I was $500.00 short I will put the other $500.00 to buy him the wristwatch and do the birthday dinner. So although he changed the plans, I was looking at the positive of still being able to do something for his birthday. I knew he was annoyed about the money decision but at least I can still put $500.00 to make up the $1000.00 I needed for his birthday present.

A couple of days later, I return home from work and my husband told me 'I put the money I owed you on your dresser but I took out the money you owe for the monthly bills. When I went to my dresser, there was $223.00. This broke me and I was completely disgusted by his actions, I recognized at that moment that he was angry and in his mood of getting me to see that I can't manage but in his anger, he completely forgot about the birthday present money and there was no way at this point that I was going to do anything for his birthday. He was out to make me pay for trying to be in control of my own money and I was just disgusted by his actions.

This was his last straw with me and after receiving the $223.00 from $1000.00 I could not stand to be in the same room as him, I could not look at him, be around him, he completely disgusted me. I know that at this point I consciously mentally left the relationship and there was no going back. The best way I can put it or explain what I mean is to say that the little switch of light that I still try to keep burning after he told me to 'PACK AND LEAVE' turned off and never came back on.

My husband's birthday came and I did nothing, I didn't even say happy birthday.

18 THE BREAK-UP

A week after his birthday, he came home one evening and I was in the bath, he said 'Beth, we need to talk about our relationship'. I replied 'ok'.

He said 'I realized that you don't talk to me anymore and we are supposed to be working on our relationship. My birthday came and you didn't do anything for me, which I know that we had decided to start and celebrate each other's birthday. I want you to reply and as you can see I am not shouting so I want you to talk because I do not know what I did you to make you hate me so much.'

I replied, 'ok let's talk about your birthday and how I

went back on what we agreed on with working on our relationship.' I decided to take charge of my own money and you got upset, took out my half, and gave me $223.00 in the end just so that I can feel the burn of taking charge of my own money. Do you really think I should have struggled to get a $1000.00 gift after you spent nearly all your gift money? Just because I decided to be in control of my own money and you were vexed so you wanted me to feel the burn!'

He replied 'oh sorry I didn't remember about the birthday money'. At this point, I shocked him because, for the first time in our relationship, I had my details down with every step accounted for; therefore, he was not able to switch up what happened to what he wants me to believe.

He continued talking by asking 'can we go for a drive to talk in private?' His sisters had moved in with us so we left our daughter with the sister that was home and we went on this drive to discuss our relationship.

He drove his car and I sat in the passenger seat. He

started 'I realized that you don't look at me anymore and any time I enter a room with you in it, your face turns like you are disgusted and then you will leave. I do not know what I have done to you for you to hate me like this, I thought we got past the 'pack and leave' that happened in January and we were working on our relationship but it seems like you don't want this anymore.' I was silent and also annoyed that he did not know what he did after what I told him about the birthday, so I said nothing at this point because with my husband, it's never his fault and it always turns on me plus there are so many apologies a person can take. Plus he completely disregarded what he did with my $1000.00.

He said 'that's another thing, you don't talk or say anything. I ask you about going for counseling, but you refuse and at this point, I don't know what to do.

I replied 'it makes no sense going counseling with you because you will overpower me, and I will be the problem so no counseling.

He replied 'do you want to break up? If we break up,

we can see other people though just so you know'.

When he said this, my brain said, 'don't give up on this chance to be free.' I replied with a quick 'ok'.

He said, 'once you are clear we can see other people'. I replied 'ok'. In my mind, I was finally free, and I didn't want to see anyone but me.

He drove us home and before we got out of the car, he took off his wedding ring and tossed it in the drink holder in the car. I guess that was supposed to make me feel bad, but I didn't react nor did I feel anyway.

He said 'you can sleep in the bedroom and I will sleep in the front house in the chairs.

The next day I woke up and a sense of freedom came over me, it was so weird. I did not feel sad nor did I cry or have any feeling to cry but instead I was happy and free. At first, I thought that I was going crazy and that I finally got mentally ill like my mother because of the joy I felt from the breakup. When I realized that I was not going crazy and I was still in my right mind, I promised myself to stay single for a very long time so that I can finally get to know myself and finally do all the things my husband did not allow me to do when we were together.

I lived with my husband for one year since we broke up and boy that was a year I would never forget.

19 AFTER THE BREAK-UP

We broke up in April 2018, and I thought we would live fine since we always lived fine together and one thing, we got right was being good roommates in the past. But when someone is out to make sure you pay for hurting them you've got another thing coming.

I started running every Saturday and then I got into strength training trying to do an actual pull-up. In the summer, I went to a few actual carnival parties.

I went back to school that same September to study Mathematics and Accounts Csecs (Caribbean Secondary

Education Certificate). I was really doing me, but hardship hit me when I had a change of position at work and was being short paid each week and did not know it. I was unable to pay my half of the bills on time plus rent. My worst week was when I got paid $36.00 after my deductions and that was the week, I had everything pile up to pay rent and bills plus food for me because we were doing everything separate. I went to my husband and asked him if he would pay the rent for me because I feel like I am being short paid and he told me 'I will let the landlord call you'. I replied, 'I told you I don't have any money so why would you have him call me?' Then I walked out because there was nothing else to say. Later on in the day while I was at work the Landlord did call and I called him back when no one was around to hear me and I explained my situation to him, he felt awful for calling me to ask for rent and said 'Ms. Parris, I am so sorry I called you for rent and it's only because your husband told me to call you saying you have the money for the rent but I apologize, so whenever you get the money you can call me'. After that day, the landlord never called me for rent but I had to always call him to come and collect.

While I was going through this financial hardship, my husband sold his car that we bought from the dealership for $55,000 with OUR money. He paid the monthly payments with OUR money and when we had only owed $23000 he took over the payment under his name alone at the credit union but our money was still doing everything else.

My husband sold that car for $18,000.00 and I asked him at the time only for $1000.00 to bring my accounts and finances up to date and he said 'when I finish pay all my bills, if any left-back and I feel to give you any, I will; if not, you are not getting a cent! That is what I got NOT ONE CENT.

Although living with my husband was becoming a challenge, I could not afford to leave and had nowhere to go. So, what I did was start to focus on building me in every other area of my life that I had control over. I did some talking with a good friend at the time and asked what my flaws were, and the reply was that I always push away good people.

I started to ask myself 'why do we push away people that are good to me?' I asked this question each day for one week and one day as I was pressing my daughter's uniform, the reply came loud and clear 'you never forgave your grandmother for dying'. When I came to this realization that I still had serious emotional wounds, I decided to heal these wounds; the best thing would be to write my grandmother a letter, read it to her, and then burn it.

The next night on my way home from work, I drove into a parking lot with my notebook and a pen and started writing like if I was talking to my grandmother in person, I poured my heart out and told her all the horrible things that happened to me after she died. I also told her why I was angry at her for dying because I felt like my life fell apart and I thought it was so unfair that she went when I was so young.

While I was writing this letter, I was crying my eyes out because I was going over wounds that I suppressed for so many years. When I finished writing, I just sat in my car and cried uncontrollably for about 1 hour straight. When I finished crying, I drove home.

The following week I went to my grandmother's grave and read out the letter to her grave, this time I took my best friend with me for emotional support. I cried a bit but not as bad as I did in the car. Finally, I got my best friend to choose a spot to go and burn the letter as a relief, we buried it in the ground and then lit it on fire and as the smoke went up, it was an experience I would never forget but I felt a relief come over me and that's the moment I finally released all that past pain.

The next task I set for myself was to love myself, so I started to do mirror work and if you don't know what that is, it's basically every time I pass a mirror, I say something I love about myself or give myself a motivational speech of how awesome I am.

As I kept working on myself, while studying, my husband started to come back and sleep on the bed in the bedroom so I moved out of the bedroom and started to sleep in my daughter's room. My husband made sure our daughter slept with him and then started to shut the door so I won't see my daughter at night when I came home and if I have to leave early in the morning. No matter what he did, I made sure I went to all my classes even with all the stress he was putting me through at home, when my exams came I passed both subjects and also recognized my love for accounting which I planned to do my ACCA (Association of Chartered Certified Accountants) next. I moved out in April 2019 because I couldn't take the living conditions with my husband and had asked the Universe/God to provide a way out of that house and I was very happy when it came through. The final thing my husband did was he went to our Human Resources Department at work the day after I moved out and told them he is going to charge me for kidnapping our daughter which if he did I would lose my job. In the end, he didn't and that was the end of him impacting my life negatively.

20 UPDATE ON MY LIFE

In January 2020, I started studying ACCA, I also started my bookkeeping business by March 2020, and I grew my YouTube channel when we were going through COVID. At present, I have 2 YouTube channels and 2 podcasts. I have built myself an online presence that I am super proud of and currently, I am working on my biggest dream.

As I come to the end of this book, I want you to use this book and pull from the strength I used knowing that you have that same strength within you. Get to know yourself and love every bit of you. If you need to get healthy, decide on a real-life plan that suits you and what you like and avoid making decisions based on what worked for someone else. This is your life, you make the decisions and if you currently don't have control to make decisions for yourself, make sure to plan for how you start taking back control because we are the ones that give our control to other people not realizing that people do things in life that suits them. So, stop living your life to please other people but please you, make sure you are happy. Your happiness comes first. Also, live your life by love; always thinking about how your actions will affect the other person because that is the true magic of living a fulfilled life.

    To this end, I want to hear from you, please share your story in the Facebook group because your story can save someone's life. Or use it to reach out for help and here are my links and email to connect with me.

Email: bethscaredtobeme@gmail.com

Facebook Group: https://www.facebook.com/groups/bebravebestrongbeyou

Instagram:

https://www.instagram.com/bebrave_bestrong_beyou/

Podcast: https://anchor.fm/bebrave-bestrong-beyou

21 YOU ARE IN CHARGE

I know my story was mostly hard, sad, and negative experiences but one thing that I must say I would not change ANYTHING that I've been through because they all made me the person I am today. Life does throw a hardball, but you have to focus on you, improve you, and ignore the negative as much as you can and focus on what you want to achieve. Don't forget to ask for what you want, be very specific on the outcome, and try your best not to try giving detail on how you will achieve your goal or change your present situation but let God/Universe decide on how you will receive it.

Make sure to forgive those people that did you wrong because it is an absolutely freeing feeling. I feel so free knowing that I have forgiven all those people that hurt me and did me wrong including my husband.

Also search within you to find that deep emotional pain that you are unconsciously dealing with and write a letter to that person, thing, or incident which you thought you released but you didn't.

If you want to follow the steps that I followed to overcome my pain with my grandmother, join my email list and I will send you the steps over the period of 5 days.

I want you to know that you have greatness within you and with your story like mine you can help so many people. We don't go through pain just because we have to but the pain, we go through happened to help you grow in some way and to teach you a lesson. So, look for the lessons in your life; appreciate the good, the bad, and the ugly.

ABOUT THE AUTHOR

Beth Parris (pen name) loves reading motivational books as this is what helped her to grow over the years. She also has a love for exercising and taking care of her health so she can be there for her daughter and see her grow up. Since she separated from her husband, she is currently enjoying her single life while focusing mainly on her career. Her favorite activity is swimming in the ocean while watching the sunset.

Printed in Great Britain
by Amazon